The Globe in Our Classroom

Declan Parnell

Rosen REAL READERS

Rosen Classroom
New York

This is our classroom.

This is our globe.

We find places on the globe.

We find states on the globe.

We find countries on the globe.

We find oceans on the globe.

Words To Know

countries

globe

ocean

states